CHOOSING TO BE A CHRISTIAN

A Study for Tweens

Abingdon Press
Nashville

CHOOSING TO BE A CHRISTIAN
A Study for Tweens

Requests for permission should be submitted in writing to Barb Porter, The United Methodist Publishing House, 201 Eighth Avenue, South, P.O. Box 801, Nashville, TN 37203; faxed to 615-749-6128; or sent via e-mail to permissions@abingdonpress.com.

Writer: Pamela Buchholz
Editor: Marcia J. Stoner
Production Editors: Janet Patterson and Theresa P. Kuhr
Designer: Randall Butler
Cover Design: Tony Kougios
Cover Photo: © Digital Juice, Inc.

ISBN 978-0-687-64741-5

09 10 11 12 13 14 15 16 17 18 — 10 9 8 7 6 5 4 3 2 1
Manufactured in the United States of America

CONTENTS

How to Use This Book 4

Session 1—Hearing the Call: One God 5

Session 2—Choosing to Follow: God Become Man 13

Session 3—Choosing to Believe: Jesus Our Savior 21

Session 4—Receiving the Spirit: Given Power to Live a Faithful Life 29

Session 5—Choosing the Church: The Body of Christ 37

Session 6—Choosing to Be a Christian: Jesus and Me .45

Additional Reproducibles 53

ABOUT THE WRITER

Reverend Pamela Buchholz is an ordained deacon and has served in the area of Christian Education for twenty-five years. She earned a M.A. in Christian Education from Garrett-Evangelical Theological Seminary and serves at First United Methodist Church in Midland, Michigan. She loves God and all of God's children.

Pam has written for Exploring Faith, Live It!, and Live B.I.G.

HOW TO USE THIS BOOK

Choosing to Be a Christian is a short-term study consisting of six (6) sessions. Sessions can be adapted from 45 minutes to an hour and a half. This study is meant to encourage tweens to explore what it means to be a Christian. It brings tweens to the understanding that becoming a Christian is a conscious choice. *Choosing to Be a Christian* exposes tweens to the corporate nature of the Christian experience.

Choosing to Be a Christian can be used as a preconfirmation curriculum that encourages tweens to take the next step of beginning the process of committing to full church membership.

Choosing to Be a Christian can be used with tweens in a variety of settings. It is designed to be used with fifth- and sixth-grade students, with optional use up to seventh grade.

SETTINGS

- Sunday school
- Wednesday nights
- Short-term studies coinciding with other short-term church events
- Study for new Christians
- Preconfirmation

USE WITH:
WHAT IS A CHRISTIAN?

The participant's piece is *What Is a Christian?* This book of puzzles, questions, and challenges is meant for use with *Choosing to Be a Christian* during the sessions. It can also be used as a stand-alone piece and makes a wonderful gift.

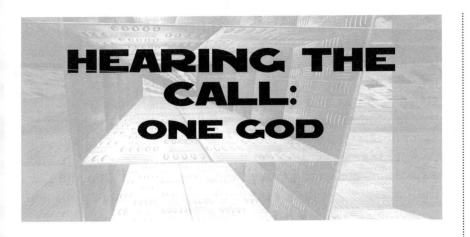

HEARING THE CALL: ONE GOD

THE MAIN IDEA

Choosing to be a Christian means choosing to worship the one, true God.

THE GOALS

Tweens will
• become familiar with the story of the calling of Abraham.
• discover different attributes of God.
• recognize that they are children of God.

THE BIBLE

Genesis 12:1-7; Deuteronomy 6:4-9; Deuteronomy 14:2

THE PLAN

Get Ready

Before there was anything, there was God. God is bigger than time and space, yet God is always near at hand. God created all that is and God continues to care for creation. Choosing to be a Christian begins with God. As Christians, we share the Jewish belief in the one, true God. This God was revealed to Abraham, the father of our faith. God is revealed to us through the Bible, through Jesus, through the record of believers who have gone before us, and through our own experience.

PREPARE YOUR SESSION

STUFF TO COLLECT:

- ❏ Bibles
- ❏ markers
- ❏ pins
- ❏ masking tape
- ❏ plain or lined paper
- ❏ pencils
- ❏ clock with a second hand or a salt timer
- ❏ candle and matches
- ❏ a rock
- ❏ a shepherd figurine (could be from a nativity)
- ❏ picture(s) of a lighthouse or other symbols associated with God
- ❏ optional: tablecloth or table runner
- ❏ **Reproducible 1A, p. 11**
- ❏ **Reproducible 1B, p. 12**
- ❏ **What Is a Christian?**

For cool ❄ options:

- ❏ **What Is a Christian?**
- ❏ paper and pencils

STUFF TO DO:

1. Make photocopies of Reproducibles 1A and 1B
2. Gather items you will need for Worship and Reflect.
3. If you plan to do the Cool Option: Adult Survey, make arrangements for tweens to visit an adult study group or class.

Being a Christian means being different. Most tweens do not want to be different from their peer group. Even rebellious teens conform to the dress and behavior of their fellow rebels. When God called the people of Israel, God called them to be a "peculiar people." They were to obey the Ten Commandments. They followed rules of worship and adopted a lifestyle that set them apart from other people. Like a good parent, God asked the Israelites to stay away from the wrong crowd. God knew that if they did not, the Israelites would be tempted to follow the idolatrous and immoral ways of the people around them.

Believing in God seems pretty obvious as a first step in choosing to be Christian. But getting to know God is a life-long journey for believers. In today's session tweens will discover through Scripture some characteristics of God. Share with them qualities of God you have experienced in your own life. Our God is a God of relationship. Knowing about God is not the same as knowing God. You can help the tweens know God by sharing stories from your own faith journey and inviting them to share ways in which they have experienced God.

GET STARTED

Get Acquainted Time: 5-10 minutes

Greet tweens as they arrive. Give each person a nametag (**Reproducible 1A, p. 11**). Tell them to complete the name-tag by filling in their favorite thing for each category listed. Be sure you and all of the adult helpers complete nametags also. When most of the tweens have arrived, give each person a "Who has the same favorite . . . ?" card. Wander around and check out one another's nametags to find who has the same favorites, filling in their names on your card.

Gather together as a group. Do a quick survey of some of the favorites. Were there any unique favorites?

That's Different Time: 10 minutes

The goal of this game is to be different. Tweens list as many names as possible in the category provided, with the goal being to list some names that no one else lists.

STUFF—GET ACQUAINTED:

❏ scissors

❏ pins

❏ masking tape

❏ pencils or markers

❏ **Reproducible 1A, p. 11**

STUFF—THAT'S DIFFERENT:

❏ plain or lined paper

❏ pencils

❏ clock with a second hand or a salt timer

CHOOSING TO BE A CHRISTIAN

How to Play:
- Hand out paper and pencils.
- Get in groups of three to six people.
- Call out one of the categories listed below.
- Give the players one minute to list as many names as they can in the category.
- Call time.
- One player in each group begins by reading his or her list of names. The other players speak up if they listed that name also, with everyone putting a check next to any names they listed that were duplicated by others. When the first player's list has been read, go around the circle with players reading any names not yet given.
- The players get a point for each unique name.

Categories:

States Starting With *M* or *T*
Men in the Old Testament
Women of the Bible
Movies About Animals
     Books of the Bible

 Teacher Tip: If you have a small class, you may choose to play this as one group.

DIG IN

Holy People   Time: 15 minutes

Hand out pencils and copies of **What Is a Christian?** Have tweens read and complete the activity, "A Holy People," on page 6. Review the answers (p. 30).

Say: If something is holy, it is something set apart from all others, different and connected with the divine. The sabbath is a holy day because it is different and set apart from all other days. It is a day to worship God and to focus on our relationship with God. It is a day connected with the divine.

Say: In Deuteronomy 14:2 the people of Israel are called holy. This does not mean that they are perfect people. It means that they are a people chosen by God and set apart for a special purpose. They are to be different from all the other people around them who worship many gods.

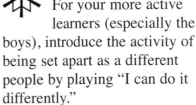 **COOL OPTION: I'm Different:**
For your more active learners (especially the boys), introduce the activity of being set apart as a different people by playing "I can do it differently."

Assign a task that must be accomplished by everybody (one at a time). The challenge is that everybody must figure out a different way to accomplish the task. Nobody may repeat how it was done by the person before them.

Example Instruction:
You must get from this wall to the wall at the other end of the room.

(sample actions: walk, run, skip, walk backward, crawl, spin, sing while walking, whistle while walking)

STUFF—HOLY PEOPLE:

❑ pencils

❑ **What Is a Christian?**

Called and Sent Time: 10-15 minutes

Hand out the pencils and **What Is a Christian?** Let tweens complete "Claimed by God" (page 7; answers, p. 30).

To learn more about Abraham read the story "Imagine That" (**Reproducible 1B, p. 12**). Then ask tweens to respond to the story by imagining how they might have felt if they had been Abraham.

Discuss the questions from the handout.

Have a volunteer read Genesis 12:1-7.

Ask: Who did God call to go to a new land? (Abram)

Say: We often refer to this new land as "the Promised Land" because it was promised to Abram (later renamed Abraham by God) and his descendants.

Ask: Do you know what that land is called today? (Israel)

Say: The land was occupied by the Canaanites when Abram and Sarai arrived. They did not go to war with the Canaanites. They shared the land with them while trying to live as a holy people, called to worship God and live in obedience to God.

Say: While we may not be called to pack up our things and move to a strange land, God does call each of us to be God's followers.

About God Time: 10–15 minutes

Say: What is God like? How can we know God? What is God's relationship with creation? These are really big questions. Asking questions and seeking understanding is part of being Christian. It is one way we can be honest with God and grow in faith.

Make sure everyone has a Bible and a copy of **What Is a Christian?** Turn to "What Is God Like?"(pages 8-9; answers, p. 30).

Divide tweens into groups of two to four. Assign each group two to four Scripture references. Tell them to read the Scriptures to learn more about the nature of God and about God's relationship with humankind.

Come back together and have them share what they learned. Are there other ways they would describe God?

 Teacher Tip: You can adapt this activity for the amount of time you have available by adjusting the number of verses each group looks up. When tweens share their responses with one another, they learn that they can do Bible study themselves.

WORSHIP AND REFLECT

Time: 5 minutes

Ask tweens to work together to create a worship center with the materials provided.

Have one of the tweens light a candle as a sign of the presence of Jesus.

Teacher Tip: Take a moment to explain to the class that the candle is a reminder of Christ's presence with us. Each week let a different tween light the candle to begin your worship time.

Draw tweens' attention to the symbols on the worship table. Explain that God is our rock, our shepherd, our guiding light, and the light in the darkness. Ask tweens to take a few minutes in silence to reflect on who God is in their lives.

Invite both tweens and adult helpers to share aloud a quality or name for God that is especially meaningful to them.

Read Deuteronomy 6:4-9.

Hand out **What Is a Christian?** and have tweens read pages 10-11, "The Shema." Read Deuteronomy 6:4-9 together. See if they can repeat 6:4 without looking. Read Deuteronomy 6:4-5 again.

STUFF—WORSHIP AND REFLECT:

- [ ] **What Is a Christian?**

- [ ] Bible

- [ ] a candle and matches

- [ ] a rock

- [ ] a shepherd figurine (could be from a nativity set)

- [ ] picture(s) of a lighthouse or other symbols associated with God

- [ ] optional: tablecloth or table runner

Teacher Tip: Sharing should be voluntary. For some tweens this is a natural thing to do, for some it can be intimidating.

Ask tweens if they know what Jesus said was the greatest commandment.

Together read "The Two Greatest Commandments" from **What Is a Christian?** page 12.

Have them compare it to "The Shema," from **What Is a Christian?** pages 10-11.

STUFF—GOD OF COVENANT:

❏ **What Is a Christian?**

❏ Bibles

❏ pencils

Say: Like other Jews, Jesus repeated this verse every morning and evening. Make a commitment this week to repeat these verses as you begin and end each day. See what difference, if any, it makes in the way you approach the events of the day.

Pray: Creator God, You have made us in your image and called us good. Help us to follow in your way and to resist temptations that would lead us into trouble. Show us how to shine our light so others will know your love through our lives. Amen.

TAKE IT FURTHER

God of Covenant Time: 10-30 minutes

Make sure everyone has a Bible. Have tweens work in pairs to complete "God of Covenant" in **What Is a Christian?** (page 13; answers, p. 30).

Come back together and compare answers.

Ask: In your relationships with family and friends, how important is it to you that people keep promises? Why?

Say: Keeping promises builds trust. The Bible shows us that God keeps promises. We can trust God to care for us.

COOL OPTION: Adult Survey:
If you have time (and there is an adult study going on at the same time), send tweens out in pairs or groups of three to survey adults in the congregation to learn how they describe God. What qualities of God are most important to them?

Reproducible 1A

NAMETAGS

Copy and cut apart the cards.
Give each person a nametag and a "Who has the same favorite . . . ?" card.

MAKE A NAMETAG

NAME

My favorite

● subject in school:

● after-school activity:

● snack:

● TV show:

WHO HAS THE SAME FAVORITE . . .

● subject in school:

● after-school activity:

● snack:

● TV show:

NAME

My favorite

● subject in school:

● after-school activity:

● snack:

● TV show:

WHO HAS THE SAME FAVORITE . . .

● subject in school:

● after-school activity:

● snack:

● TV show:

Reproducible 1B
IMAGINE THAT

Imagine that you live in the city of Ur, somewhere in what is now Iraq, around 2000 B.C. All of the people you have ever known worship many gods. You are proud of the history of your region, for it was here that writing was invented. The city is at the crossroads of trade and is an important center for economic and religious activity. This religious activity includes worship at the many shrines called "ziggurats." They are step-shaped buildings of massive stone. The staircase on the ziggurats is said to reach to the gods of heaven. Though many gods are worshiped in Ur, the moon god is considered one of the most powerful.

You live a very comfortable life. You own herds of sheep and goats. You are happily married. Though you have no children, you have a large extended family and many servants. Life is good in Ur.

Then one day you have a strange experience. You hear a divine voice speaking to you. That is amazing enough, but this god claims to be like no other. In fact, this god says he is the only God. God calls you to leave your home and take your family and flocks to a new land which God will give to you.

✱ What would you do if God told you to move to an unknown place?

✱ If everyone around you worshiped other gods, what would help you stay faithful to the one, true God?

✱ What are some ways you are "holy"—different from others because you follow God?

☞ **Read Genesis 12:1-7.**
Who did God call to leave the country of his father and go to a new land?
This man is known as the father of our faith, because he went out in faith, trusting in God.

Art: Roger Payne, Linden Artists, Copyright © 2005 by Cokesbury, *Exploring Faith: Faithzine™*, Fall 2005, p. 16.

CHOOSING TO BE A CHRISTIAN

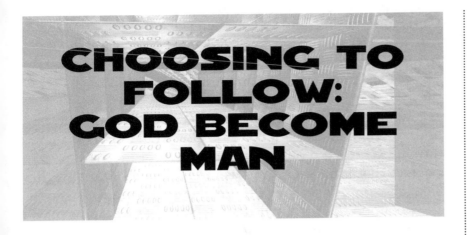

CHOOSING TO FOLLOW: GOD BECOME MAN

THE MAIN IDEA

Choosing to be a Christian means choosing to follow the teachings of Jesus.

THE GOALS

Tweens will
• be able to name some of the ways in which Jesus is shown to be fully human.
• recognize and affirm Jesus as God made flesh.
• reflect on Jesus' mission and some of his teachings and how his teachings apply to their lives.

THE BIBLE

John 1:14-18; Matthew 1:18-25; Luke 2:1-18

THE PLAN

Get Ready

Tweens find connections through personal relationships. They yearn for people who are trustworthy, caring, good listeners, and who can understand what they are going through. Whether or not they have family or friends who have these qualities, all tweens have one in their lives who does, and that is Jesus Christ.

STUFF TO COLLECT:
❑ Bibles
❑ green and yellow sheets of paper cut into fourths
❑ pens or markers
❑ pushpins or masking tape
❑ playground ball,
❑ tennis ball and Frisbee®
❑ eleven 2-liter pop bottles
❑ wastebasket
❑ large, empty coffee can or similar size container
❑ string
❑ masking tape
❑ large sheet of paper and marker, or chalkboard and chalk
❑ paper and pencils
❑ paper clips
❑ a candle and matches
❑ **Reproducible 2A, p. 19**
❑ **Reproducible 2B, p. 20**
❑ **Reproducible 2C, p. 54**
❑ **What Is a Christian?**

For cool ❄ *options:*

❑ **What Is a Christian?**
❑ Bibles and pencils
❑ green and yellow sheets of paper cut into fourths
❑ chalkboard and chalk or large sheet of paper and marker

STUFF TO DO:
1. Make photocopies of Reproducibles 2A, 2B, and 2C, and cut apart the cards.
2. Cut green and yellow paper into fourths.
3. Read the Christmas stories in the Gospels of Matthew and Luke.
4. Gather the items you will need for the Challenge Stations and set them up.

**COOL OPTION:
Nativity Knowledge
Vote:** Before the session begins, read through the Christmas stories in Matthew and Luke. Make a note of some nativity information that comes from tradition rather than the Bible. (For example, the Bible does not say how many wise men there were. The Bible does not say Jesus was born in a stable. That comes from tradition because he was laid in a manger. However, the manger may well have been in a cave.)

As tweens arrive give each two colored papers. When several have arrived, name traditional and biblical information. Have them vote by holding up the appropriate card: green—It's mentioned in the Bible; or yellow— I'm not sure.

STUFF—NATIVITY
KNOWLEDGE:

❑ green and yellow sheets of paper, cut in quarters

❑ pens or markers

❑ pushpins or masking tape

Christmas has become so commercialized and secularized that it is easy to lose the awesome message that God became a human and took on all the emotional and physical experiences that come with human existence.

A foundational Christian belief is that God "became flesh and lived among us" (John 1:14). Why would God do such a thing? God acted out of a great love for us. Jesus showed people what it meant to love as God loves. Jesus healed the sick. He spoke out against those who took advantage of the poor and the marginalized. He said that what was in people's hearts was just as important as whether or not they obeyed religious teachings. This session will help tweens discover some of the big ideas that Jesus taught. They will also gain a better understanding of what it meant for Jesus to become a man. Jesus knows how it feels to have friends turn against you, to lose someone you love, to have people make fun of you, and to experience physical suffering. When we are going through tough times, we can turn to Jesus. Jesus can comfort us and strengthen us as one who has walked this way before us.

GET STARTED

Nativity Knowledge Time: 10 minutes

As tweens arrive tell them to write down things they know about the story of Jesus' birth. If they are sure what they know is in the Bible, they write it on a green sheet of paper. If they are not sure, they write it on a yellow sheet of paper.

Have them post all of the sheets on a bulletin board or tape the sheets on the wall or chalkboard.

Ask: Where in the Bible do we find stories of Jesus' birth?
(Matthew and Luke)

Have volunteers read aloud Matthew 1:18-25 and Luke 2:1-18.

Look at the information the tweens posted and help them decide if the information is part of the biblical record or not. (Refer to Matthew 2 for information about the wise men and Luke 1 for the appearance of the angel to Mary, and Mary's visit to Elizabeth.)

Remove any sheets with incorrect information.

Wide or Narrow? Time: 10–15 minutes

Set up three challenges stations.

Challenges Station One
Set up ten of the pop bottles in a standard triangular bowling pin format. With masking tape mark a start line about fifteen to twenty feet from the front "pin." Set up the last pin in another "bowling lane," marking the start line at the same distance.

Goal: Roll a ball to knock down at least one pin. Challenge A: Stand at the start line and roll a ball to knock down the pins in the bowling pin format. Challenge B: Stand at the start line and roll a ball to knock down the one pin.

Challenges Station Two
Set an empty wastebasket and an empty coffee can a few feet apart at one end of the room. Mark a start line with masking tape about ten feet in front of the cans.

Goal: Toss a tennis ball into a can. Challenge A: Toss the ball into the wastebasket. Challenge B: Toss the ball into the coffee can.

Challenges Station Three
Use string or masking tape to mark a four-foot-diameter circle on the floor. Then mark a second circle next to it, about two feet in diameter. Mark a start line about fifteen feet in front of both circles.

Goal: Land a Frisbee® in the circle. Challenge A: Land the Frisbee® in the large circle. Challenge B: Land the Frisbee® in the small circle.

Divide the class into three groups. At each station the team will decide if they want to try for challenge "A" or "B." Successfully completing a Challenge A earns five points, and completing a Challenge B earns ten points.

When the teams have completed all three stations, gather the group back together and ask how they scored.

Ask: Did you choose the easy path that scored fewer points, or the harder challenges? Why?

Read the teaching of Jesus in Matthew 7:13-14: "Enter through the narrow gate; for the gate is wide and the road is easy that leads to destruction, and there are many who take it. For the gate is narrow and the road is hard that leads to life, and there are few who find it."

- ❏ Bibles
- ❏ playground ball
- ❏ tennis ball
- ❏ eleven 2-liter pop bottles
- ❏ wastebasket
- ❏ large, empty coffee can or similar size container
- ❏ a Frisbee®
- ❏ string
- ❏ masking tape
- ❏ paper and pencils
- ❏ **What Is a Christian?**

Teacher Tip:
If you have a small group (one to three people on a team), let everyone on the team take the challenge. If your group is large, or to save time, have each team choose one person to do each challenge.

CHOOSING TO FOLLOW

Ask: What do you think Jesus meant by entering through the narrow gate? What paths do you see young people following that seem like the easy way, but end up leading to trouble?

DIG IN

What Did Jesus Feel? Time: 15 minutes

Ask a volunteer to read John 1:14.

Say: God knew that the best way for people to know God and to understand how God wants us to live was to come and live among us. That is just what God did through Jesus Christ. Doing that meant experiencing the everyday inconveniences of life and the pain of rejection and death on the cross.

Have tweens complete the "What Did Jesus Feel?" word search in **What is a Christian?** (page 14; answers, p. 31) to discover some of the things Jesus experienced in his life.

Go over the words they found.

Ask: When might Jesus feel these feelings?

Assign individuals or groups one of the Scriptures listed at the bottom of the page. Ask them to look up the verses and share with the whole group the context of the Scripture and how Jesus felt.

The Scriptures and the topics they address are:
John 11:1-5, 28-35, 38-44—Jesus weeps, death of Lazarus
Matthew 4:1-2—Jesus is famished after fasting 40 days in the wilderness
Mark 1:12-13—Jesus is tempted in the wilderness
Matthew 21:1-11—Happiness (joy) as Jesus is proclaimed the Son of David
Matthew 21:12-13—Jesus overturns the tables in the Temple
Luke 10:38—Jesus is welcomed into a friend's home
Matthew 26:36-39—Jesus prays "let this cup pass from me"
Matthew 27:27-31, 45-50—Jesus' crucifixion

Write the word "incarnation" on the board or on a large sheet of paper. Christians speak of "God incarnate" or "the incarnation" to mean God became flesh in Jesus Christ.

❑ **What Is a Christian?**

❑ Bibles

❑ pencils

❑ chalkboard and chalk; or large sheet of paper, marker, and tape.

In the early Christian church there were people called *Docetists* who insisted Jesus only seemed to be human, but did not really feel pain or human emotion.

Ask: What difference, if any, does it make for you to know that Jesus was fully human?

 COOL OPTION: If you have time, have the tweens solve the word puzzle, "Hidden Faith Words" (page 16; answers, p. 31) of **What Is a Christian?** to reveal the words *incarnation*, *resurrection*, *salvation*, and *transformation* and talk about their meanings.

What Did Jesus Teach? Time: 10-15 minutes

Copy and cut apart the "What Did Jesus Teach?" charade slips (**Reproducible 2A and 2B, pp. 19-20**).

Play charades of what Jesus taught.

Tell the group that each slip of paper tells something that Jesus taught plus a Scripture reference.

One person will draw a slip and act out the teaching for the rest of the group to guess. The Scripture reference may help the tween act out the teaching, but it is the teaching itself the group is trying to guess. If you prefer, you may play this game as teams with one person on the team acting it out for the team to guess.

Ask: What other things can you think of that Jesus taught by his words or actions?

WORSHIP AND REFLECT

Time: 10-15 minutes

Invite a tween to light the candle as a symbol of Christ's presence with you.

Say: Our world is full of so much noise and activity, we do not take much time for quiet reflection.

STUFF—WHAT DID JESUS TEACH?:

☐ **Reproducibles 2A and 2B**

☐ Bibles

☐ scissors

STUFF—WORSHIP AND REFLECT:

☐ **What Is a Christian?**

☐ Bibles

☐ a candle and matches

☐ pencils

Have the tweens read silently the "ACTS" prayer formula (page 28) in **What is a Christian?** Then allow them five to ten minutes to write their thoughts on the spiritual journal page (page 29). Assure them that this is for their own reflection and will not be shared with the group.

When they have finished, read John 1:18.

Then have a volunteer read Matthew 28:18–20.

Say: These are Jesus' last words to the disciples before he ascended to heaven. They are words for all believers through the ages. People outside the church sometimes know very little about the life and teachings of Jesus. What are ways you can share about Jesus with others?

Close with prayer, giving thanks for God's great gift of coming to us in Jesus and God's presence with us now.

TAKE IT FURTHER

Events in Jesus' Life Time: 15 minutes

Before the session, copy and cut apart the event cards from **Reproducible 2C** (p. 54). You will need one set for every two to six people. Mix up the cards in each set and clip each set together.

Help tweens review the events of Jesus' life by working with a partner or team to put a list of events in order.

Divide the class into two or more teams.

Give each team a set of cards.

At the signal have them work together to put the events in the correct order.

Go over the order determined by the tweens, making any corrections needed. They are listed in the correct order in this leader's book.

Ask: What is the most important part of Jesus' life for you?

STUFF—EVENTS IN JESUS' LIFE:

❏ **Reproducible 2C**

❏ paper clips

❏ scissors

 COOL OPTION: Read "To Show Us the Way" in **What Is a Christian?** (page 15).

Reproducible 2A

WHAT DID JESUS TEACH?
CHARADE SLIPS

✱ Copy and cut apart the teachings cards. Teams or individuals take turns drawing a card and acting out the teaching for the rest of their team or the class to guess.

JESUS TAUGHT: FORGIVE ONE ANOTHER.

Matthew 18:21-22

Then Peter came and said to him, "Lord, if another member of the church sins against me, how often should I forgive? As many as seven times?" Jesus said to him, "Not seven times, but, I tell you, seventy-seven times."

JESUS TAUGHT: DO NOT JUDGE OTHERS.

Matthew 7:1-5

"Do not judge, so that you may not be judged. For with the judgment you make you will be judged, and the measure you give will be the measure you get. Why do you see the speck in your neighbor's eye, but do not notice the log in your own eye? Or how can you say to your neighbor, 'Let me take the speck out of your eye,' while the log is in your own eye? You hypocrite, first take the log out of your own eye, and then you will see clearly to take the speck out of your neighbor's eye."

JESUS TAUGHT: THE GREATEST COMMANDMENTS ARE TO LOVE GOD AND TO LOVE YOUR NEIGHBOR AS YOURSELF.

Matthew 22:34-40

When the Pharisees heard that he had silenced the Sadducees, they gathered together, and one of them, a lawyer, asked him a question to test him. "Teacher, which commandment in the law is the greatest?" He said to him, " 'You shall love the Lord your God with all your heart, and with all your soul, and with all your mind.' This is the greatest and first commandment. And a second is like it: 'You shall love your neighbor as yourself.' On these two commandments hang all the law and the prophets."

JESUS TAUGHT: YOU SHOW LOVE TO ME WHEN YOU CARE FOR THOSE IN NEED.

Matthew 25:34-40

"Then the king will say to those at his right hand, 'Come, you that are blessed by my Father, inherit the kingdom prepared for you from the foundation of the world; for I was hungry and you gave me food, I was thirsty and you gave me something to drink, I was a stranger and you welcomed me, I was naked and you gave me clothing, I was sick and you took care of me, I was in prison and you visited me.' Then the righteous will answer him, 'Lord, when was it that we saw you hungry and gave you food, or thirsty and gave you something to drink? And when was it that we saw you a stranger and welcomed you, or naked and gave you clothing? And when was it that we saw you sick or in prison and visited you?' And the king will answer them, 'Truly I tell you, just as you did it to one of the least of these who are members of my family, you did it to me.' "

Reproducible 2B

WHAT DID JESUS TEACH?
CHARADE SLIPS

JESUS TAUGHT: SERVE ONE ANOTHER IN LOVE.

John 13:14-17

"So if I, your Lord and Teacher, have washed your feet, you also ought to wash one another's feet. For I have set you an example, that you also should do as I have done to you. Very truly, I tell you, servants are not greater than their master, nor are messengers greater than the one who sent them. If you know these things, you are blessed if you do them."

JESUS TAUGHT: SHINE YOUR LIGHT; BE THE BEST YOU CAN BE TO GIVE GLORY TO GOD.

Matthew 5:14-16

"You are the light of the world. A city built on a hill cannot be hid. No one after lighting a lamp puts it under the bushel basket, but on the lampstand, and it gives light to all in the house. In the same way, let your light shine before others, so that they may see your good works and give glory to your Father in heaven."

JESUS TAUGHT: PRAY TO GOD.

Matthew 6:9-15

"Pray then in this way: Our Father in heaven, hallowed be your name. Your kingdom come. Your will be done, on earth as it is in heaven. Give us this day our daily bread. And forgive us our debts, as we also have forgiven our debtors. And do not bring us to the time of trial, but rescue us from the evil one. For if you forgive others their trespasses, your heavenly Father will also forgive you; but if you do not forgive others, neither will your Father forgive your trespasses."

CHOOSING TO BELIEVE: JESUS, OUR SAVIOR

THE MAIN IDEA

Choosing to be Christian means believing that Jesus is our Savior.

THE GOALS

Tweens will
• explore the Scriptures to learn Jesus' relationship to God.
• discover what they and other Christians believe about Jesus.
• recognize and affirm that we all sin and need the love of Christ.

THE BIBLE

John 1:1-14; John 3:16; Revelation 3:20

THE PLAN

Get Ready

Regardless of the time of year, decorate the room in white and gold, the liturgical colors of the Easter season. This session celebrates Jesus as Savior. It may be more difficult for tweens to connect with the divinity of Jesus than with his humanity. The amazing truth is that Jesus is both fully human and fully divine. Because of that—our God is a God who fully understands the fears, sorrows, and temptations of humanity. Be clear with tweens that Jesus is not a second God. Jesus is

PREPARE YOUR SESSION

STUFF TO COLLECT:

- ❑ Bibles
- ❑ wrapped round candies for everyone
- ❑ small soft objects (no larger than a tennis ball) to throw such as bean bags, tennis balls, or foam or squish balls (1 for every 6 tweens)
- ❑ string or masking tape
- ❑ thumbtack or tape
- ❑ pencils
- ❑ balloons (deflated)
- ❑ gardening or work gloves
- ❑ scissors
- ❑ a candle and matches
- ❑ **Reproducible 3A, p. 27**
- ❑ **Reproducible 3B, p. 28**
- ❑ **Reproducible 3C, p. 55**
- ❑ **Reproducible 3D, p. 56**
- ❑ **Reproducible 3E, p. 57**
- ❑ **What Is a Christian?**

For cool ❄ *options:*

- ❑ **What Is a Christian?**
- ❑ pencils

STUFF TO DO:

1. Make photocopies of Reproducibles 3A, 3B, 3C, 3D, and 3E. Cut any cards apart.
2. Decorate the room in white and gold, the liturgical colors for Easter.
3. Purchase wrapped candies.
4. Post targets (Reproducible 3A) on the wall and mark the start lines about nine feet away from each target.
5. Bring a pair of gardening or work gloves and several deflated balloons.

God made flesh. The first chapter of John tells us that Jesus is God and was with God from the beginning of Creation.

As our Savior, Jesus saves us from sin and death. Tweens may ask, then, why Christians still sin and die. Being a Christian doesn't make us perfect; it means our sins are forgiven. While our physical bodies will cease to exist in this world, we are promised eternal life through our faith in Jesus. Christians believe that our sin is forgiven through Jesus' death and resurrection. *Sin* may not be a word your tweens hear much. They may wonder how we can be both "good" and sinners. The definition in the session of sin as "missing the mark" may help tweens broaden their understanding of sin beyond just doing something wrong. Though there is always more we could do to follow Christ more perfectly, the good news we have as Christians is that our sins are already forgiven and we are "children of God" and "heirs to the kingdom" (Romans 8:16, 17). Though Jesus as Savior can be a challenging subject, you will convey this best by sharing what it means to you to have Jesus as Lord of your life.

GET STARTED

Find the Beginning Time: 5–10 minutes

Have tweens stand in a circle with their hands behind their backs. Choose one person to be in the middle (IT). Explain that the beginning of this circle is the person who is holding a round object. It is the task of IT to find that person.

The object is passed from person to person, behind their backs. To make it more challenging, everyone pretends to be passing the object. Give IT two chances to guess correctly. Then have IT switch places with another player and start a new round. Each time you start a round, have IT close her eyes while you place the object in someone's hands.

Mix things up completely on the final round by placing objects in lots of people's hands or even in everyone's! When IT makes a guess, ask everyone to show their object.

Read John 1:1-5.

Ask: Who does John say was there in the beginning with God? (Jesus) **When was the beginning?** (at creation)

Read Revelation 22:13 from the Bible. Explain that *alpha* is the first letter in the Greek alphabet and *omega* is the last.

Ask: What does it mean to you that Jesus is "the first and the last, the beginning and the end"?

Say: Christians believe that there is no beginning or end to God. God always was and always will be. When Jesus says that he is "the first and the last, the beginning and the end" it is a way of saying that he always was and always will be.

On Target   Time: 10 minutes

Post each target, **Reproducible 3A** (p. 27), on a wall and mark a start line about nine feet back from each target.

Tweens line up in front of the target. Each person gets three throws. Post one person near the target to judge whether or not the thrower hits the "perfection" circle.

When everyone has had a turn, gather together as a group.

Ask: How many had three perfect throws? Who had even one or two perfect throws?

Say: In life, as in this game, we sometimes miss the mark. We fail to fully worship God and live in love and peace with one another.

Ask: What are some small ways we miss the mark? (Ask tweens to consider how responsible they are in doing things without being reminded and whether or not they always treat everyone with kindness and consideration. Do they stand up for those who are bullied or who are ignored by peers?)

Say: Christians believe that Jesus died to save us from sin. The word *sin* means more than just doing something wrong. The New Testament actually uses five different Greek words for the word that we translate as *sin*. The word used most often is a word that is best translated as "missing the target," a term also used in relation to archery. Who can say that they never "miss the target" in terms of their words, actions, or thoughts?

Read John 3:16.

STUFF—ON TARGET:

❑ **Reproducible 3A**
   (1 for every 6 tweens)

❑ Bibles

❑ thumbtack or tape

❑ small, soft object (no larger than tennis ball) to throw such as bean bag, tennis ball, or foam or squish ball (1 for every 6 tweens)

❑ string or masking tape

Say: Because of Jesus' death and resurrection, our sins are not counted against us. The cross is the big eraser that erases forever the record of those sins.

DIG IN

What I Believe   Time: 15–20 minutes

Have tweens turn to "What I Believe" in **What Is a Christian?** (page 19). Invite tweens to respond honestly to each statement. Is this something they believe, don't believe, or aren't sure about?

Do a quick survey of the class. Read each statement and ask them to raise a hand to show whether they believe it, don't believe, or are not sure.

Say: There are a variety of beliefs within the world of Christendom. Faithful Christians can and do have different understandings about the origin of the Bible and about the historical truth of all events in the Bible. That does not mean, however, that you can believe anything and still be a Christian. While there is a wide spectrum of belief among Christians, some key beliefs that all Christians share are:

Faith in Jesus to save and transform lives.
Belief that Jesus is divine like God.
Belief that God was revealed to us through Jesus, that God became man.
Belief that Jesus died on the cross and was resurrected, as witnessed by many of his followers.
Belief that Jesus lives in us through the Holy Spirit.
Belief that through Jesus, we also will have eternal life.
Belief that we are called and helped to follow in the way of Jesus, loving God and loving neighbor.

Read John 1:14.

Say: Christians understand that Jesus is the living Word of God. While Christians may differ in their understanding of the Bible, all Christians agree that the Word of God made known in Jesus reveals the way God wants us to live and offers us fullness of life.

❏ **What Is a Christian?**

❏ pencils

Teacher Tip:
You know your class best. If you do not think your tweens will feel comfortable honestly sharing their responses with one another, skip this step.

Who Is Jesus? Time: 15-20 minutes

We can know who Jesus is through the Bible and our own experiences. Discover more about the nature of Jesus and his relationship with humankind by reading Scripture.

Make sure everyone has a Bible and a pencil. Hand out "Discovering Jesus," **Reproducible 3B** (p. 28). Depending on the time, have each tween read and respond to two or more of the Bible passages.

Discuss their responses. Things we learn from Scripture include:
1. John 1:1 Jesus and God are one and Jesus has existed since the beginning.
2. Luke 3:21-22: Jesus is God's Son and God was pleased with him.
3. Luke 4:16-21: Jesus is the fulfillment of prophecy. He came to bring healing and justice.
4. Matthew 15:29-31: Jesus had power to heal and his good works led people to praise God.
5. John 3:16: Jesus proves God's love. Because Jesus lived and died and rose again, all who believe will have eternal life.
6. 2 Corinthians 5:17: Having Jesus in our lives changes us.

Say: One way we know about Jesus is from the Bible. We can also know Jesus through our own experiences.

Share some ways you have experienced Jesus. Invite tweens to share times they have experienced Jesus in their lives.

WORSHIP AND REFLECT

Time: 5-10 minutes

Invite a tween to light the candle as a symbol of Christ's presence with you.

Lay the gloves and balloons, deflated, on the worship table.

Ask the tweens if they have ever been to a party that was decorated with deflated balloons.

Say: Balloons don't function as balloons until they are filled with air. You would never take someone a bouquet of deflated balloons to cheer them up!

COOL OPTION: Encourage tweens to solve the "Coded Message" in **What Is a Christian?** (page 18). Talk about what it means that Jesus is "the bread of life."

STUFF—WORSHIP AND REFLECT:

❏ Bible

❏ balloons

❏ gardening or work gloves

❏ a candle and matches

Pick up the gloves and Say: Although this is a work glove, it won't accomplish any work unless there is a willing hand inside it. Like the balloons, when we are filled with Christ, we have a new spirit of joy and are able to offer hope and comfort to others. Like the gloves, when Jesus comes into our lives, we are given strength to face challenges and do the work of caring for ourselves and others. (*Read Revelation 3:20.*)

Say: Jesus wants to come into our lives. All we have to do is say, "Yes, we want you to fill our lives." If you have never asked Jesus to come into your life, I invite you to do that today during our prayer time. If Jesus is already part of your life, take this time to recommit yourself to trusting in him and following in his way. (*Lead the group in prayer.*)

Pray: Loving God, thank you for sending Jesus into the world so we could know you better. Even though we know how you want us to live, sometimes we do things our own way. Forgive us for times we have knowingly or unknowingly hurt others. Forgive us for times we have missed opportunities to show your love. Lord, we open the doors of our hearts and invite you in. Thank you for your love and care, and your promise to be with us always; in Jesus' name we pray. Amen.

TAKE IT FURTHER

Symbols of Jesus Time: 15-20 minutes

Before the session photocopy and cut apart the Symbols of Jesus Matching Game Cards, **Reproducibles 3C, 3D, and 3E** (pp. 55-57).

Lay the cards out facedown on a table. Play a traditional matching game, only you are trying to match the symbol with its meaning. Each player turns over two cards. If the symbol and meaning match, he keeps the cards and plays again. If the cards do not match, he turns the cards back down and the next person's turn begins. The symbols used in this game tell us about Jesus' life and some of the names for Jesus.

Say: The Bible tells us a lot about Jesus; but the symbols Christians use to remind them of Jesus, tell us some things about Jesus, too.

Ask: What do you think the most important thing you know about Jesus is? (Jesus is our Savior. Accept all reasonable answers.)

STUFF—SYMBOLS OF JESUS:

❑ **Reproducibles 3C, 3D, and 3E, pp. 55-57**

❑ scissors

Teacher Tip: If you have a large group, let them play as partners working together to turn over and match cards, or make more than one set of cards and set up multiple games.

CHOOSING TO BE A CHRISTIAN

Reproducible 3A
TARGET

● Copy the target and post it on a wall. You will need one target for every six tweens.

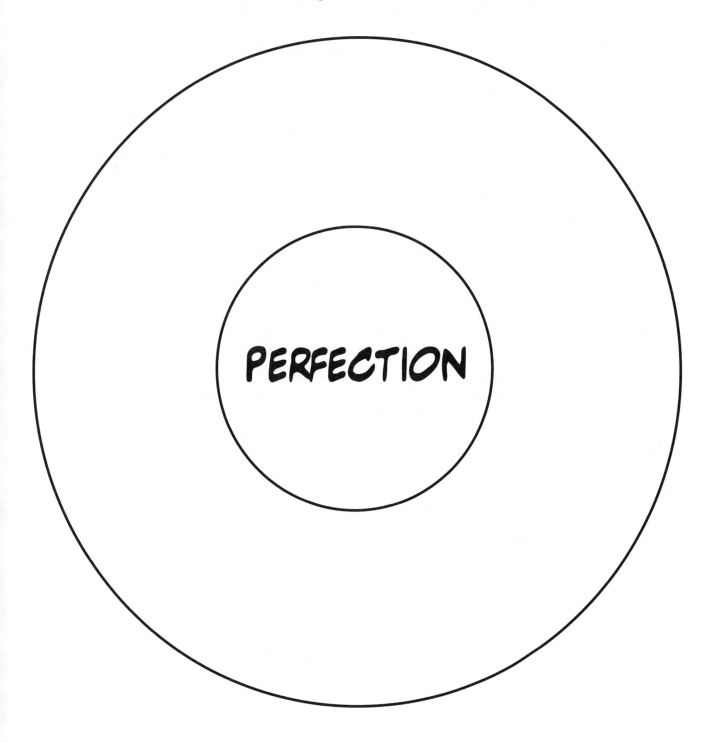

Reproducible 3B
DISCOVERING JESUS

👉 Read each Scripture.
What does that verse tell you about Jesus?

JOHN 1:1

In the beginning was the Word, and the Word was with God, and the Word was God.

LUKE 3:21-22

Now when all the people were baptized, and when Jesus also had been baptized and was praying, the heaven was opened, and the Holy Spirit descended upon him in bodily form like a dove. And a voice came from heaven, "You are my Son, the Beloved; with you I am well pleased."

LUKE 4:16-21

When he came to Nazareth, where he had been brought up, he went to the synagogue on the sabbath day, as was his custom. He stood up to read, and the scroll of the prophet Isaiah was given to him. He unrolled the scroll and found the place where it was written: "The Spirit of the Lord is upon me, because he has anointed me to bring good news to the poor. He has sent me to proclaim release to the captives and recovery of sight to the blind, to let the oppressed go free, to proclaim the year of the Lord's favor." And he rolled up the scroll, gave it back to the attendant, and sat down. The eyes of all in the synagogue were fixed on him. Then he began to say to them, "Today this scripture has been fulfilled in your hearing."

MATTHEW 15:29-31

After Jesus had left that place, he passed along the Sea of Galilee, and he went up the mountain, where he sat down. Great crowds came to him, bringing with them the lame, the maimed, the blind, the mute, and many others. They put them at his feet, and he cured them, so that the crowd was amazed when they saw the mute speaking, the maimed whole, the lame walking, and the blind seeing. And they praised the God of Israel.

JOHN 3:16

"For God so loved the world that he gave his only Son, so that everyone who believes in him may not perish but may have eternal life."

2 CORINTHIANS 5:17

So if anyone is in Christ, there is a new creation: everything old has passed away; see, everything has become new!

CHOOSING TO BE A CHRISTIAN

RECEIVING THE SPIRIT: GIVEN POWER TO LIVE A FAITHFUL LIFE

THE MAIN IDEA

Choosing to be Christian means receiving the gift of the Holy Spirit who gives us the power to live more and more in the way of Jesus.

THE GOALS

Tweens will
- recognize that the Holy Spirit is a gift sent to guide and help us.
- connect with the story of how Peter was changed by the Holy Spirit.
- recognize and affirm that the Holy Spirit is available to all who believe.

THE BIBLE

John 14; Acts 2; 2 Corinthians 5:17

THE PLAN

Get Ready

The Holy Spirit arrived in a dramatic way on the Day of Pentecost. The writer of Acts tries to tell us what happened through a series of word pictures. There was a "sound like a violent wind" and "tongues, as of fire." The Holy Spirit filled Jesus' followers, giving them a new sense of purpose and the courage to take action. Christians celebrate Pentecost as

STUFF TO COLLECT:

- ❏ Bibles
- ❏ paper, pencils, tape
- ❏ adhesive nametags or squares of paper
- ❏ markers and crayons
- ❏ 8 folding chairs
- ❏ 2 sheets of red paper
- ❏ cloth for two blindfolds
- ❏ candles and matches
- ❏ CD player
- ❏ CD of contemplative Christian music
- ❏ red balloons/streamers
- ❏ **Reproducible 4A, p. 35**
- ❏ **Reproducible 4B, p. 36**
- ❏ **Reproducible 4C, p. 58**
- ❏ **Reproducible 4D, p. 59**
- ❏ **What Is a Christian?**

For cool ❄ *options:*

- ❏ cake mix and necessary ingredients to add
- ❏ tub(s) of frosting
- ❏ hand mixer or large spoon
- ❏ measuring cup
- ❏ large bowl
- ❏ cake pans or muffin tins
- ❏ potholders
- ❏ knives

STUFF TO DO:

1. Make photocopies of Reproducibles 4A, 4B, 4C, and 4D.
2. Purchase nametags or cut them out of paper.
3. Set up two obstacle courses in a different area from where you first gather.
4. If you choose to do the Cool Options: Bake a Cake, buy the ingredients and gather the necessary utensils.
5. Bring a CD of contemporary Christian music.

the birthday of the church, but Pentecost was celebrated by Jews since Old Testament times as a spring harvest festival. In Acts 2 we read that Jerusalem was crowded with Jews from many nations who had come to worship on Pentecost.

With the coming of the Holy Spirit, we see the disciples transformed from fearful, silent people to people who boldly proclaim the good news of Jesus as Lord and Savior. The same Peter who denied Jesus for fear of his life stands up and preaches a sermon with an invitation to be baptized. That invitation is accepted by over 3,000 people. From that time on, Jesus' followers went about preaching and baptizing.

Red is the liturgical color of Pentecost, symbolizing the tongues of fire described in Acts. This session is about transformation (change), so set the tone for the day by transforming your room with red balloons and/or streamers.

Pentecost is a story for today. It assures us that Jesus will send us the Holy Spirit too. Tweens can identify with the feelings of fear and confusion that the disciples experienced. The good news is that the same Spirit who gave courage and direction to the disciples is available to us.

GET STARTED

STUFF—WHO AM I?:

- ❏ Bibles

- ❏ adhesive nametags or squares of paper and tape

- ❏ markers

Who Am I? Time: 10 minutes

Have everyone write their name on a nametag. Collect the nametags and mix them up.

Have tweens stand in a circle, with everyone facing the back of the person on their right. Give each person a nametag, not letting anyone see it. Tell them to stick the nametag on the back of the person in front of them.

Then ask them to mingle around the room, asking "yes" and "no" questions to discover whose nametag they are wearing. Explain that at first they may not ask any questions related to physical appearance. Instead, they will need to ask questions about the person's interests, gifts, and relationships. This will be challenging for groups who do not know one another well.

See how many can guess who they are. Then, if necessary, allow them to ask questions related to physical appearance, such as height, color of clothing, and hair color.

Come back together for discussion.

Ask: Was it easy or difficult for you to discover your identity? Why?

Read 2 Corinthians 5:17.

Say: We each have unique gifts given by God. Jesus helps us use our gifts to be more like him. Jesus promised to send his followers the Holy Spirit. The Holy Spirit is God within us, helping us to grow into faithful disciples. This transformation is possible because of the Holy Spirit at work in us.

Obstacle Race Time: 5–10 minutes

Tape a sheet of red paper on the back of two chairs. Use chairs to make two identical obstacle courses with the red chairs at the end.

Ask for two volunteers to be blindfolded. Invite a third person to assist one of the blindfolded volunteers. Tell the volunteers to move around the obstacles and take a seat in the chair with red paper on it. One person will not have anyone to provide assistance, while the other person will be led by a helper. As soon as one person is seated in the correct chair, call time.

Let the blindfolded volunteers tell how they felt about the experience. Did they feel like they knew where they were going? Were they unsure? Was it fair to have a guide for one person, but not the other?

Ask everyone to complete the "Transformation" puzzle in **What Is a Christian?** (page 22; answers, p. 31).

Say: We think of an *advocate* as someone who stands up for us. In the Bible, it is one of the words used for the Holy Spirit. Jesus knew that when he left this earth, his followers would feel lost, alone, and afraid. He promised not to abandon them. He told them he would send the Holy Spirit to guide, comfort, and strengthen them. Without the Holy Spirit, we are like the person who was blindfolded and left with no guide. Though we cannot know all that lies ahead, when we pay attention to the nudgings of the Spirit of God within us, we can follow in the way Jesus wants us to go.

STUFF—OBSTACLE RACE:

- ❏ **What Is a Christian?**
- ❏ pencils
- ❏ 8 folding chairs
- ❏ 2 sheets of red paper
- ❏ tape
- ❏ cloth for two blindfolds

Teacher Tip:
If possible, have the obstacle courses set up in a different area from where you first gather. If this is not possible, do not arrange the chairs until the first participant is blindfolded.

STUFF—THREE IN ONE:

- ❏ Bibles
- ❏ pencils
- ❏ **Reproducible 4A**
- ❏ **Reproducible 4B**

COOL OPTION: Bake a Cake. Explain that Pentecost is celebrated by Christians as the birthday of the church. Once Jesus' followers received the Holy Spirit, they were emboldened to spread the good news that Jesus is our Lord and Savior. Within one generation Christianity spread throughout the Roman Empire.

Make a birthday cake, following the directions on any cake mix. Have tweens take turns adding ingredients and mixing the batter. Pour the batter into a cake pan or muffin tin and bake. Before the end of the session let the tweens frost and eat the cake.

STUFF—TRANSFORMED BY THE SPIRIT:

- ❏ Bibles
- ❏ **Reproducibles 4C and 4D**

Three in One Time: 15 minutes

Read John 14:15-18.

Jesus says these words at the Last Supper. Later, just before Jesus ascends into heaven, Jesus tells the disciples to wait in Jerusalem for the gift of the Holy Spirit.

To learn more about the relationship between God, Jesus, and the Holy Spirit, read together "Three In One" (**Reproducible 4A**, p. 35). Give tweens a few minutes to fill in the missing words on the Trinity symbol and to decide what they think the descending dove symbol represents. Invite them to share their responses.

Say: **Some people name the Trinity as Father, Son, and Holy Spirit, and some people name it for their actions: Creator, Redeemer, and Sustainer. Jesus is God with us and the Holy Spirit is God within us, but as Christians we believe in only one God.**

Ask tweens to complete, "Lost in Translation" (**Reproducible 4B,** p. 36).

Say: **The Greek word for Holy Spirit is *Paraclete*** (PEAR–uh–klete). **It can be translated in at least four different ways. Unscramble the letters to learn the meanings of the word *Paraclete*.** (Answers: Comforter, Counselor, Advocate, and Helper.)

Ask: **What do you think of when you hear the word *comforter? counselor? advocate? helper?* What difference do you think it made to the disciples to have Jesus send them the Holy Spirit?**

Transformed by the Spirit Time: 15 minutes

Say: **Imagine how you would feel if your very best friend disappeared. Imagine if that friend was also your teacher and a person who guided you every day. That was the situation for the disciples when Jesus was crucified. Even though they'd seen the risen Lord, they felt lost and afraid without Jesus there to lead them. Just before Jesus ascended** to heaven he told the disciples to wait in Jerusalem. Just as he had promised, Jesus would not leave his followers alone. He would send them the Holy Spirit.

Hand out the copies of "An Amazing Transformation" (**Reproducibles 4C and 4D**, pp. 58 and 59).

Assign parts. Give the readers a few minutes to silently look over their parts

Read Acts 1:4-5.

Have the readers present "An Amazing Transformation," Parts One and Two.

Ask: How did the Holy Spirit change Peter?

Say: Imagine that you are one of the people questioning Peter in the courtyard after Jesus was arrested. From your meeting with Peter, what might you think of Jesus?

Say: Imagine that you are in the crowd on Pentecost. After your encounter with Peter, what might you think of Jesus?

Read 2 Corinthians 5:17.

Say: Peter, the disciples, the people in the crowd at Pentecost, and all believers were transformed by the power of the Holy Spirit sent by Jesus Christ.

Share with your tweens ways you have experienced the Holy Spirit guiding you or encouraging you. Invite them to think of times they have heard an inner voice urging them to do or not do something. Could this be the Holy Spirit at work? Are there other times they have felt the comfort or guidance of the Holy Spirit?

Teacher Tip: Ask for six volunteers to read the parts of the Narrator, Peter, Servant Girl, Person 1, Person 2, and the Rooster in "Part One: Peter Denies Jesus." Then assign six people to join Peter and the Narrator to read the parts of John, Mary, Voice 1, Voice 2, Voice 3, and Voice 4 in "Part Two: Peter Transformed." (**Reproducibles 4C and 4D**, pp. 58 and 59).

Teacher Tip: For a small group, readers can read more than one part. You might take a part yourself.

WORSHIP AND REFLECT

Time: 5 –10 minutes

Gather in a worship space that can be darkened. Before moving to the worship space ask tweens to come to the worship area in silence. Play a CD of Christian contemporary music that will encourage prayerful reflection, and dim the lights.

STUFF—WORSHIP AND REFLECT:

❏ candles, matches

❏ CD player and CD of contemplative Christian music

Say: Sometimes we feel like we live in a world of darkness. We feel hopeless. We can't see any way out. We don't know where we're going or where all of this may lead.

(Light the candles.)

Say: But Jesus offers us hope. Jesus fills our lives with the light of his love through the Holy Spirit.

Invite the tweens to join in a prayer litany by responding with, "Fill me with your Spirit, Lord."

Leader: With rushing wind and flaming tongues,
All: Fill me with your Spirit, Lord.

Leader: When the darkness of night lasts through the day,
All: Fill me with your Spirit, Lord.

Leader: When I lose my way and forget your way,
All: Fill me with your Spirit, Lord.

Leader: When I'm so afraid of tomorrow, I cannot live today,
All: Fill me with your Spirit, Lord.

Leader: When I feel alone, even in the middle of a crowd,
All: Fill me with your Spirit, Lord.

Leader: Wake me up, lift me up, fill me up, and send me forth.
All: Fill me with your Spirit, Lord. **Amen.**

TAKE IT FURTHER

Dramatic Presentation Time: 30 minutes

Ask tweens to divide (as evenly as possible) into four groups according to their preferred style of presentation: rap/song, television drama, art, or commercial. Each group will take a part of the Pentecost story and retell it in their group's format (see sidebar). Allow groups about 20 minutes to prepare. Then have each group present their part of the biblical story.

Ask: Did these presentations help you see anything new in the Bible message? What does the story of Pentecost mean for believers today? What difference, if any, does the Holy Spirit make in your life?

STUFF—DRAMATIC
PRESENTATION:

❏ Bibles

❏ paper and pencils

❏ crayons and markers

1. Acts 1:1-5 and 12-14 (rap/song)
2. Acts 2:1-4 (art)
3. Acts 2:5-15 (drama)
4. Acts 2:22-24; 37-38 (commercial)

Reproducible 4A
THREE IN ONE

ONE CREATOR

Since the early years of the church, people have studied the Scriptures to better understand the relationship between God the Creator, Jesus, and the Holy Spirit. From the time of Abraham it is clear that there is only one God who created the world and continues to care for us. The first commandment says: "You shall have no other gods before me."

ONE SON

Yet, Christians believe that Jesus is also divine. In Matthew 16:16, Peter declares this truth: "You are the Messiah, the Son of the living God." So, if we worship only one God, how can Jesus also be divine?

ONE SPIRIT

In the Gospel of John, Jesus promised not to leave his followers alone, but to send his Spirit to live within them. If there is only one God, how can there be a divine Spirit within us?

THREE IN ONE

The *Trinity* is the word Christians use to describe the relationship between God the Creator, Jesus, and the Holy Spirit. That word is not found anywhere in the Bible. Although our faith is founded on Scripture, it is also informed by tradition, experience, and reason. Centuries of thinking about God (tradition), personal experience, and reason lead us to understand that there is one God, revealed to us in three ways. We know God as our Father and Creator, as our Savior through Jesus, and as our Sustainer through the Holy Spirit.

This symbol represents the Trinity. In the center loop write the word "God." In each of the other loops write the name of one aspect of God.

▶ **Which part of the Trinity is represented by the following symbol?**

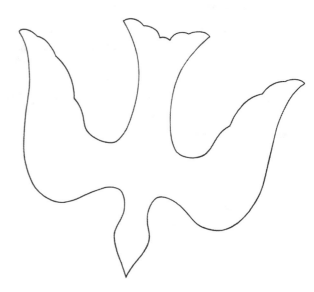

▶ **Read Luke 3:21-22 to learn one of the stories behind this symbol.**

Art: Florence Davis, Copyright © 2001 Abingdon Press, *Symbols of Faith*, pp. 45, 102.

Reproducible 4B
LOST IN TRANSLATION

👉 Jesus assures his followers that he will not leave them alone. He promises to send believers the Spirit to live in them. The New Testament was written in Greek. The Greek word for spirit is *Paraclete*. It can be translated in four different ways in English. Unscramble the letters to find four meanings of Paraclete.

C R E O F M O T R   _ _ _ _ _ _ _ _ _

O L N S O R E C U   _ _ _ _ _ _ _ _ _

C O T V A E D A   _ _ _ _ _ _ _ _

P R E E L H   _ _ _ _ _ _ _

◆ Look back at the list of meanings for *Paraclete*.

◆ What difference do you think it made to the disciples to have Jesus send them the Holy Spirit?

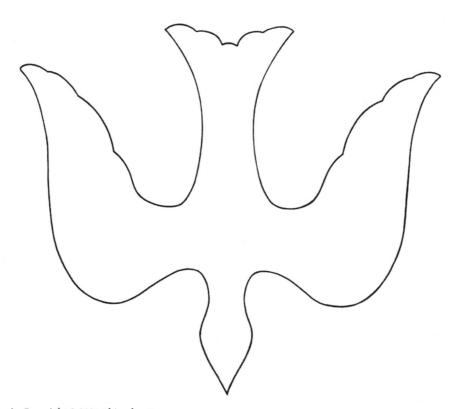

Art: Florence Davis, Copyright © 2001 Abingdon Press,
Symbols of Faith, p. 45.

    CHOOSING TO BE A CHRISTIAN

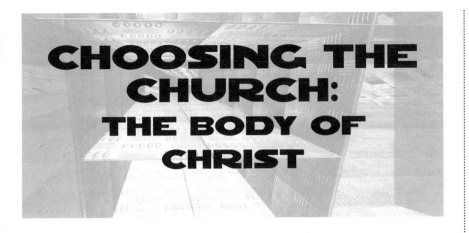

CHOOSING THE CHURCH: THE BODY OF CHRIST

THE MAIN IDEA

Choosing to be Christian means choosing to be part of the body of Christ, the church.

THE GOALS

Tweens will
• hear what it means to be part of the body of Christ.
• recognize and affirm some of their own God-given gifts.
• discover practices of the New Testament church and identify ways those are found in the church today.
• identify ways they can use their gifts to serve Christ through the church.

THE BIBLE

Matthew 28:19-20; Acts 2:37-42; Romans 12:4-8; 1 Corinthians 12:27.

THE PLAN

Get Ready

God gives all of us gifts. The Holy Spirit gives us the power to use those gifts to praise God and to serve others as the body of Christ. Being Christian is not meant to be a solo activity. From the beginning of Christianity, we see the church named as the body of Christ. In other words, it is through this body of believers that the work of Christ continues to be done.

STUFF TO COLLECT:
- [ ] Bibles and pencils
- [ ] scissors
- [ ] heavyweight paper or cardstock
- [ ] crayons or markers, including red, blue, green, yellow, and orange.
- [ ] chalkboard and chalk; markerboard and dry-erase markers; or large sheets of paper, markers, and masking tape
- [ ] optional: hymnals
- [ ] a candle and matches
- [ ] **What Is a Christian?**
- [ ] **Reproducible 5A, p. 43**
- [ ] **Reproducible 5B, p. 44**
- [ ] **Reproducible 5C, p. 60**
- [ ] **Reproducible 5D, p. 61**
- [ ] **Reproducible 5E, p. 62**

For cool ❄ *options:*
- [ ] **What Is a Christian?**
- [ ] Bibles and pencils
- [ ] church bulletins
- [ ] small plaques (one per tween and adult)
- [ ] paintbrushes
- [ ] colorful paper
- [ ] small bowls/white glue
- [ ] craft sticks
- [ ] several damp cloths

STUFF TO DO:
1. Make photocopies of 5A, 5B, 5D, 5E (Reproducibles).
2. Photocopy 5C onto heavyweight paper or cardstock; cut out the puzzle pieces.
3. Check your marker supply.
4. If you do the Cool Option: Gift Plaques, purchase small plaques for each tween, adult, and visitor.
5. Gather items needed to promote the "Personal Care Sunday." (see p. 42)

COOL OPTION: "Gifts Plaques." Make reminders of the gifts of each group member.

Purchase small plaques to decoupage from a local craft store.

Have tweens glue the "four gifts" they chose in "Gifted by God" to colorful pieces of paper, and then glue them onto their plaque.

Dilute white glue with water as your decoupage medium. Use paintbrushes to spread the glue over the "gifts." Use craft sticks to smooth out any wrinkles. Use a damp cloth to remove excess glue.

Allow to dry thoroughly. The plaques probably will need to dry until next session.

STUFF—GIFTED BY GOD:

❏ **Reproducibles 5A & 5B**

❏ scissors

Being Christian is all about relationships; our relationship with God through Christ, our relationship with other believers through the church, and our relationship with the world as Christ's servants.

This is all very countercultural. Our society tends to be "me" focused. Tweens are measured on their individual achievements and encouraged to push to achieve personal goals. The media says that if you don't make the cut, you'll be voted out. As Christians, we have the assurance that all people are persons of worth and all gifts are important. Personal achievements are great, but as Christians we can accomplish so much more when we unite as a church. Not only can we serve more needs, but we also have the strength of others to help us where we are weak, and the faith of others to nurture us in our own spiritual walk.

Consider ways you can move beyond talk to putting your faith into action. Work together as a group to support a mission project of your church or to promote the "Personal Care Share Sunday" described in the session (see p. 42). As tweens get involved in service, they will experience what it means to be the church, the body of Christ.

GET STARTED

Gifted By God Time: 10 minutes

Make copies of "What Are Your Gifts?" (**Reproducible 5A & 5B**, pp. 43 and 44) for each tween and adult helper.

Break into groups of three to six with adult leaders participating along with the tweens.

Have each person cut out four gifts they feel they might have.

After allowing time to think and make choices, ask everyone to place their four choices in front of them for everyone to see. Do not question anyone's choices, but celebrate the different gifts each person has.

Look at how many different gifts your group has. Ask each group to count the number of different gifts for its group.

Bring everyone back together and compare the number of gifts in each group.

Say: This is not a contest. Rather, we have been given gifts to use for the glory of God and the needs of the community of faith.

Read Romans 12:4-8.

Say: Paul wrote these words in a letter to the Christians in Rome to help them appreciate one another and use the gifts of all to build up the church. You can buy a box of candy at the store, but it is not a gift unless you give it away. Through the Holy Spirit we have all been given gifts. They are given to us to use in service to the world.

Look at each person's gifts and help them name ways they can use them to build up the church and serve Christ.

All the Pieces Time: 10–15 minutes

Copy the puzzle "Pieces of the Whole" (**Reproducible 5C**, p. 60), preferably onto heavyweight paper or cardstock. Cut the pieces apart. Mark the back side of each puzzle piece with an X.

Give each tween and adult helper a piece of the puzzle. Every person is to write his or her name on the front of the puzzle piece along with one of his or her gifts. If there are extra pieces, ask tweens to write the names of other persons in the church and a gift those persons bring on the remaining puzzle pieces.

Work together to assemble the puzzle. When you are done read the verse on the puzzle, 1 Corinthians 12:27.

Say: A church is not a building. A church is people. What difference, if any, would it make if we no longer had this church building or meeting space? What could we do to still be the church without a church building?

DIG IN

The Church In Action Time: 15 minutes

Give everyone a copy of "The Church in Action" (**Reproducible 5D**, p. 61), a Bible, and a pencil.

Say: The things we do as a church were not just made up by a committee back in the early history of the church.

COOL OPTION: Have tweens read Galatians 5:22. Then challenge them to find the nine Fruit of the Spirit in "The Holy Spirit" word search in **What Is a Christian?** (page 23; answers, p. 32). Ask them how these qualities might demonstrate God's love to others.

STUFF—ALL THE PIECES:

- ☐ **Reproducible 5C**
- ☐ heavyweight paper or cardstock
- ☐ scissors
- ☐ markers

Teacher Tip: If you anticipate having more than 24 participants, make a second copy of the puzzle in another color.

STUFF—THE CHURCH IN ACTION:

- ☐ **Reproducible 5D**
- ☐ Bibles
- ☐ pencils
- ☐ chalkboard and chalk, or large sheets of paper, markers, and masking tape

Teacher Tip: If time or reading levels are an issue, have tweens in each group divide the readings still further, or divide tweens into pairs and assign one Scripture to each pair.

COOL OPTION: Puzzle: Let the tweens solve the "Scrambled Tiles" puzzle in **What Is a Christian?** (page 26, answer p. 32). Then read together the verse from 1 Corinthians 12:27.

STUFF—A CLOSER LOOK:

❑ crayons or markers, including red, yellow, blue, orange, and green (for each tween)

❑ pens

They are based on the actions of the New Testament church. These first Christians were living out the teachings and practices of Jesus. Read the Scriptures listed on the handout. For each, write down things it says the church does.

Have half of the group begin at the top of the list and the other half begin at the bottom. Give them five minutes to read and record as much as possible. At the end of that time alternate between the two groups, inviting persons to share what they learned. As they share, have someone record the responses on the board or on a large sheet of paper.

Possible Responses—actions and descriptions of the early church include:

Acts 2:38: Repentance, baptism in the name of Jesus Christ for the forgiveness of sins, receiving the Holy Spirit
Acts 2:42: Hearing the Word proclaimed, fellowship, the Lord's Supper, and prayers
Romans 15:25-26: Giving to the poor
1 Corinthians 11:23-26: Celebrating Holy Communion
1 Corinthians 14:26: Worship includes: hymns, a lesson, a revelation, a word from God (tongue), or an interpretation; all for building up the faith
Colossians 4:2: Pray
James 2:14-18: Put faith into action

Ask: What other things, if any, does our church do?

Read Matthew 28:19-20. **Say:** These words were spoken by Jesus just before his ascension to heaven. They are Jesus' commandment to his followers. This was his plan for carrying on his mission: go, teach, baptize, make disciples.

Ask: How do you think we as Christians are doing in carrying out Jesus' plan?

A Closer Look Time: 10 minutes

Explain that a worship service, whether traditional or contemporary, usually contains certain basic elements. Turn to "Called to Worship" in **What Is a Christian?** (pages 24-25; answers–p. 32).

Tell the tweens to use the colors indicated to highlight each part of the worship as found in the order of service in **What Is a Christian?**

Ask: In our church, what elements are found most often? Are there any elements we are missing? What part of our worship service is most meaningful to you? Why? (Some may not know which is most meaningful. That's okay.)

How's Your Spirit?   Time: 15 minutes

Give everyone a copy of "How's Your Spirit?" (**Reproducible 5E**, p. 62) and ask them to complete the evaluation. The adult leaders should complete the evaluation also. The first part of the evaluation asks questions related to the group as a whole. The second part is a personal reflection. The last section asks the group to think about changes they can make individually and as a group to grow as Christians and live more faithfully.

Without pressuring anyone to reveal more than they feel comfortable with, invite the group to share their responses. For each statement, ask the adults and tweens to raise their hand if they answered with a one or a two, a three, or a four or a five. Everyone may not reveal their answer on every question, but record the totals you do receive to get a general feel for the group's spiritual temperature.

Discuss the final two questions. Are there things the group could add or do differently to improve the Christian atmosphere and help everyone grow in faith? What could you do to strengthen your personal spiritual life?

WORSHIP AND REFLECT

Time: 5-10 minutes

Invite a tween to light the candle as a symbol of Christ's presence with you.

Since the early church, one of the things the gathered community did was sing hymns. If you have hymnals, sing or read aloud the words to "I Am the Church" or "Forward Through the Ages." Otherwise, sing a praise song the group knows.

Let a volunteer read Ephesians 4:4-6.

STUFF—HOW'S YOUR SPIRIT?:

❏ **Reproducibles 5E**

❏ white markerboard and dry-erase markers or large sheets of paper and markers

❏ pencils

STUFF—WORSHIP AND REFLECT:

❏ Bibles

❏ optional: hymnals

❏ a candle and matches

Teacher Tip: If you have less mature tweens or new Christians, they may not be ready to ask someone to pray for them. Judge by how responsive your tweens have been to this point.

If they are not ready, skip the sharing with one another and just ask them to say a general prayer for the person on their right during silent prayer.

STUFF—A SERVANT PEOPLE:

- ❑ Bibles
- ❑ posterboard
- ❑ construction paper
- ❑ markers
- ❑ large boxes
- ❑ bulletin board paper
- ❑ bulletin board border
- ❑ stapler and staples
- ❑ Optional: computer
- ❑ Optional: copy paper

Say: One of the important things we do as the body of Christ is to pray for one another and for the world.

Have tweens turn to the person next to them. If possible, have the partners spread out so they can have a more private, quiet space for sharing. Tell them to turn to their partners and share one thing they would like their partners to pray about for them.

Come back into one circle. Begin with a word of prayer for the group and then allow several moments for a time of silent prayer in which they may pray for one another. Close with the Lord's Prayer.

TAKE IT FURTHER

A Servant People Time: 20-40 minutes

Read Matthew 25:34-40.

Ask: What does this Scripture say that the church should be doing? What are ways our church serves people in need?

Promote a "Personal Care Share Sunday" on which members of the congregation are asked to bring in care items such as toothbrushes, toothpaste, laundry detergent, soap, and shampoo for distribution to those in need.

While your class could do this project on their own, it will be more effective if the church works together. Coordinate this project with your pastor and missions chairperson.

Determine how the items will be distributed. This could be done through a local social-service agency, your own church, a school, or a soup kitchen. If possible, set the collection date for the last day of your sessions. If you have access to a computer, some students could design a flyer about the project.

Things To Do:
Make posters.
Write bulletin announcements.
Make flyers to be reproduced and distributed.
Write a brief skit for announcement time in worship.
Make a bulletin board.
Decorate and label containers for collecting the items.

Reproducible 5A
WHAT ARE YOUR GIFTS?

caring

trustworthy

helpful

creative

dependable

optimistic

strong

modest

generous

loving

Reproducible 5B
WHAT ARE YOUR GIFTS?

peacemaker

thoughtful

forgiving

patient

honest

understanding

bold

wise

gentleness

just

faithful

cheerfulness

open-minded

persistent

leadership

CHOOSING TO BE A CHRISTIAN

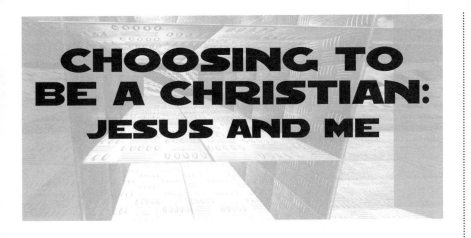

CHOOSING TO BE A CHRISTIAN: JESUS AND ME

THE MAIN IDEA

Choosing to be Christian means asking Jesus to be at the center of your life and committing to follow him.

THE GOALS

Tweens will
• know that faith is from God.
• recognize that they must choose whether or not to be a Christian.
• learn some elements of and experience prayer.
• look at choices they make every day in following Christ.

THE BIBLE

Matthew 5:13-16; John 3:1-16

THE PLAN

Get Ready

We all make choices every day. Some choices are small, like what we will wear or what we will eat. Other choices are life changing. The most important choice a person can make is the decision to follow Jesus. While God claims each person as a valuable child of God, God also created us with free will. It is up to us, enabled by God's grace, to accept the love and forgiveness God offers us through Jesus Christ. It is up to us to choose whether or not to be Christian.

PREPARE YOUR SESSION

STUFF TO COLLECT:

❑ Bibles
❑ scissors
❑ pencils
❑ candles and matches
❑ chalkboard and chalk; markerboard and dry-erase markers; or large sheets of paper, markers, and masking tape
❑ **Reproducible 6A, p. 51**
❑ **Reproducible 6B, p. 52**
❑ **Reproducible 6C, p. 63**
❑ **Reproducible 6D, p. 64**
❑ **What Is a Christian?**

For cool ❄ *options:*

❑ **What Is a Christian?"**
❑ **pencils**

STUFF TO DO:

1. Make photocopies of Reproducibles 6A, 6B, 6C, and 6D, and cut apart any cards. You will need two sets of 6A.

You can help your tweens understand that once we decide to become Christians, the hard work of living as a Christian begins. Choosing to be a Christian is a daily choice. How will we respond to that person who annoys us? Will we go along with something that is harmful to us or others just because our friends are doing it or because it offers some momentary thrill? How will we grow in our faith? How will we take the love of Christ to the world?

In this individualistic society, your tweens may misunderstand Christianity as simply a personal choice. While it is a decision each individual must make, our Christian faith is lived out through the community of the church. It is there that we worship God and join with others to serve the world in the name of Christ. Even prayer is not just about our individual relationship with God. We pray for others, asking God to give them strength, guidance, and healing.

Take time to invite the tweens to ask any questions they wish. Do not be afraid to say, "I don't know" and to seek guidance from your pastor and the Bible. Assure them that they will always have some unanswered questions. That is a sign of a Christian who continues to seek to know God more.

GET STARTED

Who's Your Leader? Time: 7–10 minutes

Stand in a circle. Choose one person to be IT. Send IT out of the room and choose another person to be the leader. The leader will start a series of actions for the group to imitate. The group is to respond so quickly, without looking directly at the leader, that it is difficult to figure out who the leader is. Before calling IT back in, give the leader a minute to think of several different actions.

Have IT return and stand in the center of the circle. Explain that the group will be following a leader, doing whatever the leader does. IT will have two chances to guess who is the leader. Then choose another IT and another leader.

Ask: Was it hard to guess who the group was following? In real life, can you think of times when it is easy to tell who a group of kids is following? What things have you done, either good or bad, because you've seen others doing them? Is there anything you do that would show others that you are following Jesus?

❏ none

Teacher Tip: Actions might include, stamping a foot, snapping fingers, nodding the head, waving a hand, and so forth.

Bible Zone Time: 10–15 minutes

Copy and cut apart the Bible question cards (**Reproducible 6B, p. 52**). Make two sets of the disciple cards (**Reproducible 6A, p. 51**). Cut them apart and stack each set together so that "Me" is the bottom card.

Read Matthew 5:13-16.

Say: Jesus said we are to be salt of the earth. Salt is valued for the flavor it adds to food and for its ability to keep food from spoiling. We are to be salt, that is, we are to add flavor to life and to keep the world from evil. Jesus also said we are to be a light to the world. God has given us gifts. We are not to hide them under a basket, but to use them so that others might give glory to God.

The question Christians need to ask is, "How can we be salt and light?" The Bible is the "how-to" manual for Christians. It is the record of our faith history and the main source of our understanding of who God is and how God wants us to live.

This Bible quiz is a chance to review some teachings from the Bible. (The answer is printed at the bottom of each card.)

Directions for Bible Quiz Time:

Divide into two groups, "Salt" and "Light."

The leader draws a question card (**Reproducible 6B**) and reads it to the Salt Team. If the Salt Team answers correctly, they get two disciple cards. If they miss, the question is repeated to the Light Team. If the Light Team answers correctly, they get only one disciple card. The Light Team then gets another question to begin the next round. The goal is to collect all of the disciple cards (**Reproducible 6A**).

Have the winning team read off the names of the disciples.

Say: Jesus called twelve disciples to follow him, learn from him and carry on his mission. Besides these twelve, the Bible tells us of many others who followed Jesus. The invitation is also for us. We are also called to be Jesus' disciples. One way to become more faithful disciples is to read and study the Bible. Some people stop with that, but being Christian means both knowing the Word and living the Word.

❏ **Reproducible 6A**

❏ **Reproducible 6B**

❏ scissors

Teacher Tip: There are thirteen disciple cards, not twelve. The thirteenth card says "Me."

DIG IN

- **Reproducible 6C & 6D**
- Bibles
- pencils

What Does It Take? Time: 20 minutes

Photocopy and cut apart the cards for "What Does It Take?" (**Reproducible 6C and 6D,** pp. 63-64). Divide into three groups: Action Faction, Faith Alone, and Membership Counts. Make sure everyone has a Bible.

Give each group the cards with their group's Scripture readings, emphasizing one way to of living as a Christian. Allow groups about ten minutes to read the Scriptures and decide how they will present what they learned.

After the presentations, **ask: Having heard what everyone learned, what do you think it means to be a Christian?**

Read Ephesians 2:8. **Ask: Is salvation our work or God's work?** (God's)

Say: We come to faith by the grace of God, not by our own efforts. Salvation is God's gift through Jesus Christ. Our good works in the world are our response to God's love. Jesus knew it would be tough to be a Christian alone. He also knew that to really make a difference in the world, it takes people with different gifts working together. The Bible refers to the church as "the body of Christ." Membership in a church does not make us Christian, but it does give us a community through which we can experience God in worship, study the Bible together, and serve the world. God is the starting point. We know God's love through Jesus. We receive salvation through Jesus' death and resurrection. We accept that gift of salvation by faith. We come to faith by the grace of God, and so, have come full circle.

A New Spirit Time: 15 minutes

Have tweens do "Bible Math" in **What Is a Christian?** (p. 27). When they are done, read the verse, John 3:16.

Ask: Why do you think this is called the heart of the Gospel? Say: This verse is really the punch line to a talk Jesus had with a man named Nicodemus. Nicodemus was a Jew. The Bible calls him a Pharisee. That means he took God's law very seriously. In fact, most Pharisees took the commandments so

- **What Is a Christian?**
- Bibles
- pencils

seriously that they cared more about obeying the law than about loving God and neighbor.

Read the story of Nicodemus in John 3:1-16.

Ask: Why do you think Nicodemus came to Jesus at night? (perhaps so the other Pharisees would not know) What did Jesus tell Nicodemus he had to do to enter the kingdom of God? (be born again) What do you think of when you hear the expression "born again"?

Say: Jesus meant that we need a change of heart, a new spirit. Some people come to know Jesus and have a dramatic change in their lives. Other people can't remember a time when they didn't know Jesus. While they still make a conscious choice to follow Jesus, they may not be able to name a particular time when this happened.

Take this opportunity as the teacher to share how you became a Christian and what it means for you to follow Jesus.

Gather in a circle for prayer. Give thanks to God for sending Jesus into the world. Ask God for forgiveness, allowing a time for silent prayers of confession. Invite any who have not done so before to ask Jesus to be Lord of their lives. Ask for guidance through the Holy Spirit to help all follow in the way of Jesus as they choose to be Christian.

WORSHIP AND REFLECT

Time: 10 minutes

Ask for a volunteer to light the candles.

Say: By God's grace we are claimed as God's children and offered salvation through Jesus Christ. We have a choice to make. Will we accept Christ as our Savior and choose to follow him? Choosing to be a Christian is something we do each day as we decide how we will use our time and our gifts, as we decide how we will relate to other people, and most of all, as we decide whether or not to pursue a closer relationship with God through prayer, worship and study. Choosing to be a Christian is a lifetime commitment of daily seeking to grow closer to Jesus. Being a Christian

STUFF—WORSHIP AND REFLECT:

❑ Bibles

❑ candle and matches

Leader: For God so loved the world

All: For God so loved the world

Leader: that he gave his only Son,

All: that he gave his only Son,

Leader: so that everyone who believes in him

All: so that everyone who believes in him

Leader: may not perish

All: may not perish

Leader: but may have eternal life.

All: but may have eternal life.

STUFF—TALKING WITH GOD:

❏ Bibles and pencils

❏ large sheets of paper and markers, or chalkboard and chalk

COOL OPTION: Seven Day Challenge. Hand out **What Is a Christian?** and turn to "Seven-day Challenge," pages 28-29. Read through the ACTS model of prayer.

Stress that this is just one model, but it can help us to keep prayers from being just a wish list for God. Challenge tweens and adult helpers to use this model and the questions asked for a week, perhaps writing in a prayer journal to begin or strengthen the practice of daily prayer. Talking to God and listening to God daily are practices that will help us grow in faith as we choose to be Christian.

does not mean we are perfect. It means we desire to more perfectly love and serve our Lord.

Invite tweens to share, as they are ready, something they believe about Jesus or a way they know Jesus in their lives.

Have volunteers read Matthew 5:14-16 and John 3:16.

Ask: What do those verses say to you?

Close by saying John 3:16 in an echo litany. (see sidebar)

TAKE IT FURTHER

Talking With God Time: 15 minutes

Say: Prayer is central to being Christian. Imagine meeting a new friend and then never having any more contact with that person; not talking to the person, not writing, and not instant messaging. If we want to develop a relationship with someone we need to be in contact with the person by talking to the person and listening to the person. The same is true with a relationship with God through Jesus Christ.

Draw two columns on large sheets of paper or a chalkboard. Label one column "friends" and the other "parents." Brainstorm things tweens talk to their friends about and things they talk to their parents about.

Ask: Do you only talk to your friends to ask them to do something for you? Do you only talk to your parents to ask them for something?

Say: If we want to build a relationship with someone, we talk to them about all the things that are important in our lives. If you are a good friend, you will rejoice when your friend rejoices. A good relationship is a two-way one. You listen to your friend and your friend listens to you. Too often the relationship people have with God is one way and one topic. Prayer can become just me telling God what God should do for me. That would not make for a very good relationship with a friend or parent, and it does not make for a good relationship with God.

DISCIPLE CARDS

JAMES, SON OF ALPHAEUS	SIMON PETER	ANDREW
JAMES, SON OF ZEBEDEE	JOHN	PHILIP
BARTHOLOMEW	THOMAS	MATTHEW
JUDAS ISCARIOT	THADDAEUS	SIMON THE ZEALOT
	ME	

Reproducible 6B
BIBLE QUESTIONS

The first book of the Bible is
_____.
A: Genesis

The Bible is made up of two main parts. They are_____.
A: Old Testament and the New Testament

The word *Gospel* means
A: good news

The four books known as the Gospels are:
A: Matthew, Mark, Luke and John

Who baptized Jesus and prepared the way by calling people to repent?
A: John the Baptist

"The Lord is my shepherd, I shall not want" is the beginning of which Psalm?
A: Psalm 23

What town was King David's hometown and the birthplace of Jesus?
A: Bethlehem

God spoke to this person from a burning bush and told him to set his people free.
A: Moses

The first Christians gathered together for
a. prayer
b. singing hymns
c. Communion
d. fellowship
A: all of the above

Jesus sometimes answered a question by telling a parable. What is a parable?
A: a story that teaches a lesson

When Paul says we are the body of Christ he is talking about _____.
a. the church
b. communion bread
c. priests
A: the church

This word means that God, Jesus and the Holy Spirit are three aspects of one God:
a. Pentecost
b. Unitarian
c. Trinity
A: Trinity

What did Jesus promise to send his followers after he was gone?
A: the Holy Spirit

Name all of the following that describe the Holy Spirit:
a. comforter
b. advocate
c. guardian angel
A: a and b

Jesus especially cared for
a. the people in power
b. the outcast
c. little children
A: b and c

Which disciple denied Jesus three times, but on Pentecost preached a sermon that brought thousands to Jesus?
A: Peter

The book of the Bible that tells the history of the early church is:
a. Philippians
b. Revelation
c. Acts
A: Acts

Jesus commanded his disciples to go and
a. make disciples
b. baptize
c. teach his word
A: all of the above

John 3:16 says that God so loved the world he:
A: gave his only Son

Which of the following do Christians believe about Jesus?
a. was a person with real feelings
b. had the power of God
c. willingly died on the cross
A: all of the above

For Christians, the important thing is:
a. how we treat others
b. that we trust in Jesus
c. our style of worship
A: a and b

CHOOSING TO BE A CHRISTIAN

ADDITIONAL

REPRODUCIBLES

Reproducible 2C
EVENTS IN JESUS' LIFE

☞ **Make a copy of this page for every two to six tweens in your group. They are shown here in the correct order. Cut apart each set of events, mix them up and clip them together for each group.**

◆ Jesus is born in Bethlehem.

◆ Jesus is baptized by John in the River Jordan.

◆ Jesus calls twelve disciples.

◆ Jesus goes about teaching and healing.

◆ Jesus is greeted as a king with palms and shouts of "Hosanna!"

◆ Jesus shares his Last Supper with the disciples during Passover.

◆ Jesus prays in the garden of Gethsemane.

◆ Jesus is arrested.

◆ Jesus is condemned to die by Pilate, the Roman governor.

◆ Jesus is crucified between two thieves.

◆ Jesus dies and is placed in a tomb.

◆ Women visit the tomb and find it empty.

◆ The resurrected Jesus appears to his followers.

◆ Jesus sends the Holy Spirit to comfort and give courage to believers.

Reproducible 3C
JESUS SYMBOL MATCHING CARDS

✳ **Manger:** Symbol of birth of Jesus, the Messiah.

✳ **Palm Branch:** Symbol of Jesus' triumphal entry into Jerusalem. "Hosanna to the Son of David! Blessed is the one who comes in the name of the Lord!" (Matthew 21:9)

✳ **Basin and Towel:** Symbol of servanthood. Reminds us Jesus washed the disciples' feet.

✳ **Crown of Thorns:** Symbol of Jesus' suffering on the cross.

✳ **Baptismal Shell:** Symbol of baptism. Three drops of water symbolize the Holy Trinity.

Manger

Palm Branch

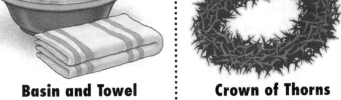
Basin and Towel

Crown of Thorns

Baptismal Shell

Art: Randy Wollenmann, Copyright © 2008 Cokesbury, *Rock Solid: Tweens in Transition, Annual Resource Pak 2008–2009*, pp. 23 and 25.

Reproducible 3D
JESUS SYMBOL MATCHING CARDS

◆ **Bread and Cup:** Symbol of Communion. Symbol of Jesus' sacrifice for us. Represents his body and blood. We are to remember Jesus during Communion.

◆ **Cross:** Symbol of Jesus' crucifixion and death. The empty cross is a symbol of Jesus' resurrection. Main symbol of Christianity.

◆ **Butterfly:** Symbol of the Resurrection and eternal life. Symbol of the transformation Jesus brings to our lives.

◆ **Bread:** Symbol of Jesus, the bread of life. (John 6:35)

◆ **Shepherd's Staff:** Symbol of Jesus, the Good Shepherd. (John 10:11)

Bread and Cup

Cross

Butterfly

Bread

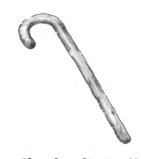

Shepherd's Staff

Art: Randy Wollenmann (bread, cup, cross), Copyright © 2008 Cokesbury, *Rock Solid: Tweens in Transition, Annual Resource Pak 2008–2009*, p. 25. (Butterfly and shepherd's staff) Copyright © 2009 Cokesbury.

Reproducible 3E
JESUS SYMBOL MATCHING CARDS

✱ Alpha and Omega: Symbol of God's power. God is first and last, beginning and end. When used with the cross, it stands for Jesus, who was with God at the beginning and is with God now. (*Alpha* and *Omega* are the first and last letters of the Greek alphabet. Here they are combined.)

✱ IHE: Symbol of Jesus. It's an acrostic of the five Greek words for Jesus Christ, Son of God, Savior.

✱ Star: Symbol of Jesus, the light of the world. (John 8:12)

✱ Chi Rho: Symbol of Jesus. It is a monogram of Jesus' name. (*X* and *P* are the first two letters of the Greek word for Christ. Put together they make the Chi Rho.)

✱ Sheep: Symbol of Jesus, the Lamb of God. Represents Jesus' sacrifice of himself on the cross.

Alpha and Omega

IHE

Star

Chi Rho

Sheep

Art: Randy Wollenmann, Copyright © 2004 and © 2008 Cokesbury.
Art (IHE): Florence Davis, Copyright © 2001 Abingdon Press.
Art (sheep): © Art Explosion.

Reproducible 4C
AN AMAZING TRANSFORMATION

Part One: Peter Denies Jesus (Based on Luke 22:54-62)

Speakers: Narrator, Peter, Servant Girl, Person 1, Person 2, Rooster

Narrator: What a night! Jesus was arrested in the garden of Gethsemane, betrayed by one of his own disciples. There was a brief struggle between the temple guards and the other disciples, but Jesus ordered them not to resist. As the temple guards took Jesus away, the disciples scattered into the night. Only one disciple followed Jesus in the shadows to the home of the high priest. When Jesus was taken inside for a hearing, that one disciple, Peter, waited in the courtyard for news of Jesus. He knew it was a dangerous place at a dangerous time, but as often was the case for Peter, he listened to his heart and not his head. Peter was standing by the fire when a servant girl spotted him.

(*Servant girl enters*)

Servant Girl: Say, you, by the fire. You were with that man, Jesus, weren't you?

Peter: Woman, where do you get off saying that? I don't even know him.

Servant Girl: Is that so? Whatever you say.

Person 1: Hey, you. Aren't you one of those following Jesus?

Peter: No, I'm not. I'm not one of them.

Person 2: Surely, you are. I can tell you're from his part of the country. You have a Galilean accent.

Peter: Man, I don't even know who you're talking about!

Rooster: Cock-a-doodle-doo.

Narrator: Peter ran off, weeping bitterly. He remembered how Jesus had warned him earlier that day, "Before the cock crows, you will deny me three times."

Reproducible 4D
AN AMAZING TRANSFORMATION

Part Two: Peter Transformed (Based on Acts 2)

Speakers: Narrator, Peter, John, Mary, Voice 1, Voice 2, Voice 3, and Voice 4

Narrator: After the Crucifixion and Resurrection the disciples waited in Jerusalem as commanded by Jesus. They stayed in the upper room and went out only when necessary. No one wanted to be the next person arrested by the Romans. They waited in Jerusalem for fifty days, until the Day of Pentecost. Pentecost was a Jewish harvest festival, a time to thank God for the gift of the spring harvest and to remember God's gift of the Law. Little did anyone know that the meaning of Pentecost was about to change forever for followers of Jesus.

Peter: It's Pentecost. We should be celebrating.

John: Instead we're here, hoping the Romans will forget about us. Hey, what's going on? Did someone leave the door open? There's a terrific wind blowing through here.

Mary: I hear the sound of the wind, but I feel the warmth of a fire. It's like I have tongues of fire on me. I'm going out on the porch.

Peter: Let's all go out and see what is going on. What a crowd is out here! There must be Jews from every corner of the world here to celebrate Pentecost. Remember how Jesus said we should go and tell the good news to all of the nations? Why have we been so fearful? The world needs to know Jesus like we do!

(a voice from the crowd)

Voice 1: Aren't you Jesus' disciples? Why aren't you speaking Hebrew? I can't understand a word you're saying! Are you drunk?

Peter: We're not drunk! For goodness sake, it's only nine o'clock in the morning! Yes, of course, we are Jesus' disciples.

Voice 2: I can understand you perfectly, but how did you learn my language? I'm from Mesopotamia.

Voice 3: No, he's speaking my language, and I'm Egyptian.

Voice 4: What's going on here? He's speaking in my language, and I'm from Rome.

Peter: Listen! Don't you see? Prophecy is being fulfilled today. The Spirit has come upon us. It's just like Jesus promised. Jesus, the one you handed over to the authorities, is the Son of God. He was crucified on a cross, but God raised him up on the third day. We are all witnesses to his resurrection. Jesus has been exalted by God and now he has poured out his Spirit upon us.

All Voices: What should we do?

Peter: Repent, and be baptized in the name of Jesus. Your sins will be forgiven and you will receive the Holy Spirit.

Narrator: Fearful Peter was transformed into Peter the Bold that day by the power of the Holy Spirit. Because of his witness, three thousand people heard the truth about Jesus and were baptized. We celebrate Pentecost as the birthday of the church because on that day the disciples received the Holy Spirit and were empowered by God to tell the good news that Jesus is our Lord and Savior.

Now you are the

body of Christ and

individually

members of it.

1 Corinthians 12:27

Reproducible 5D
THE CHURCH IN ACTION

SCRIPTURE	WHAT THE CHURCH DOES
Acts 2:38	
Acts 2:42	
Romans 15:25-26	
1 Corinthians 11:23-26	
1 Corinthians 14:26	
Colossians 4:2	
James 2:14-18	

Reproducible 5E
HOW'S YOUR SPIRIT?

☞ Rate the following statements, 1 to 5, with a one being <u>Always</u> and a five being <u>Never</u>.

❊ THE GROUP   1 2 3 4 5

One or two people make the decisions.

Prayer is important to our group.

We look for ways to be of service.

We are welcoming of new people.

We bring new people to the group.

We accept different ways of understanding Scripture.

❊ JUST YOU   1 2 3 4 5

I participate regularly in worship.

I read the Bible at home.

I talk about my faith with people outside of church.

I pray daily.

When I'm not sure what to do, I sometimes seek advice from trusted Christians.

I make an effort to treat others as I'd like to be treated.

❊ WHAT'S NEXT?

What is one thing the group could do to better act as the body of Christ?

What is one change the Holy Spirit might help you make in your life?

Reproducible 6C

WHAT DOES IT TAKE? PART 1

 Copy and cut apart the cards. Give one category of cards to each group.

Based on the Scriptures on their card, put together a presentation telling the
others what they need to do to be a Christian.

▲ **ACTION FACTION**
They will know we are Christians by our love!

Philippians 4:8-9
Finally, beloved, whatever is true, whatever is
honorable, whatever is just, whatever is pure,
whatever is pleasing, whatever is commendable,
if there is any excellence and if there is anything
worthy of praise, think about these things. Keep
on doing the things that you have learned and
received and heard and seen in me, and the God
of peace will be with you.

▲ **MEMBERSHIP COUNTS**
The church is the body of Christ, so to be Christian
you must be part of the body.

Ephesians 4:4-6
There is one body and one Spirit, just as you were
called to the one hope of your calling, one Lord,
one faith, one baptism, one God and Father of all,
who is above all and through all and in all.

▲ **MEMBERSHIP COUNTS**
The church is the body of Christ, so to be Christian
you must be part of the body.

1 Peter 3:21-22
And baptism, which this prefigured, now saves
you—not as a removal of dirt from the body, but
as an appeal to God for a good conscience, through
the resurrection of Jesus Christ, who has gone into
heaven and is at the right hand of God, with angels,
authorities, and powers made subject to him.

▲ **ACTION FACTION**
They will know we are Christians by our love!

James 2:14-17
What good is it, my brothers and sisters, if you
say you have faith but do not have works? Can
faith save you? If a brother or sister is naked and
lacks daily food, and one of you says to them,
"Go in peace; keep warm and eat your fill," and
yet you do not supply their bodily needs, what
is the good of that? So faith by itself, if it has no
works, is dead.

▲ **ACTION FACTION**
They will know we are Christians by our love!
Matthew 25:34-40

"Then the king will say to those at his right hand,
'Come, you that are blessed by my Father, inherit the
kingdom prepared for you from the foundation of the
world; for I was hungry and you gave me food, I was
thirsty and you gave me something to drink, I was a
stranger and you welcomed me, I was naked and you
gave me clothing, I was sick and you took care of me,
I was in prison and you visited me.' Then the righteous
will answer him, 'Lord, when was it that we saw you
hungry and gave you food, or thirsty and gave you
something to drink? And when was it that we saw you a
stranger and welcomed you, or naked and gave you
clothing? And when was it that we saw you sick or in
prison and visited you?' And the king will answer them,
'Truly I tell you, just as you did it to one of the least of
these who are members of my family, you did it to me.'"

CHOOSING TO BE A CHRISTIAN

Reproducible 6D

WHAT DOES IT TAKE? PART 2

▲ MEMBERSHIP COUNTS
The church is the body of Christ, so to be Christian you must be part of the body.

1 Corinthians 11:23-26
For I received from the Lord what I also handed on to you, that the Lord Jesus on the night when he was betrayed took a loaf of bread, and when he had given thanks, he broke it and said, "This is my body that is for you. Do this in remembrance of me." In the same way he took the cup also, after supper, saying, "This cup is the new covenant in my blood. Do this, as often as you drink it, in remembrance of me." For as often as you eat this bread and drink the cup, you proclaim the Lord's death until he comes.

▲ FAITH ALONE
We are saved by faith in Jesus Christ. Being a Christian is all about what you believe.

Romans 3:22-24
…the righteousness of God through faith in Jesus Christ for all who believe. For there is no distinction, since all have sinned and fall short of the glory of God; they are now justified by his grace as a gift, through the redemption that is in Christ Jesus.

▲ FAITH ALONE
We are saved by faith in Jesus Christ. Being a Christian is all about what you believe.

1 Thessalonians 5:9
For God has destined us not for wrath but for obtaining salvation through our Lord Jesus Christ.

▲ FAITH ALONE
We are saved by faith in Jesus Christ. Being a Christian is all about what you believe.

John 3:16
"For God so loved the world that he gave his only Son, so that everyone who believes in him may not perish but may have eternal life."